Contents

ACKNOWLEDGEMENTS

I am indebted to the Home Board, the Social and Moral Welfare and the Overseas Mission and Inter-Church Relations Departments of the Church of Scotland, and to members of their staff, for permission to use photographs.

COVER PHOTOGRAPH: *The Old Town of Edinburgh. By kind permission of The Church of Scotland Home Board.*

The Church of Scotland

by
James Bulloch

FOREWORD BY
THE RT REVD PROF. THOMAS F. TORRANCE

A Division of Pergamon Press

A. Wheaton & Company,
A Division of Pergamon Press
Hennock Road, Exeter EX2 8RP

Pergamon Press Ltd,
Headington Hill Hall, Oxford OX3 0BW

Pergamon Press Inc,
Maxwell House, Fairview Park, Elmsford, New York 10523

Pergamon of Canada Ltd,
75, The East Mall, Toronto, Ontario M8Z 2L9

Pergamon Press (Australia) Pty. Ltd,
19a, Boundary Street, Rushcutters Bay, N.S.W. 2011

Pergamon Press GmbH,
6242 Kronberg/Taunus, Pferdstrasse 1,
Frankfurt-am-Main, West Germany

First edition 1977

Printed in Great Britain by A. Wheaton & Co., Exeter
ISBN 0 08 021188 7 net
ISBN 0 08 021187 9 non net

Foreword

Many accounts of the Church of Scotland, long and short, have been written, but in none of them does the historical heritage of the Kirk come so vividly and relevantly before us as in this remarkable little book by the Reverend Dr James Bulloch, who has been minister of the ancient parish of Stobo for over twenty years. He is the finest of Church historians, who carries his great learning lightly. He writes not from a detached academic outlook but out of the heart of long personal experience in the actual parish, so that in what he provides in the following pages the ancient tradition remains alive as a dynamic force in the present. With wise selection he concentrates on the essential elements of our chequered history, and brings it before us finely interwoven with the distinctive Scottish emphases on faith and worship, congregation and presbytery, Church and State: and yet it is all given its proper place within the One Holy Catholic and Apostolic Church and its universal mission to bring the Gospel to all mankind. Thus while providing young people with real insights into the Presbyterian character of the Church of Scotland, far from being narrow or merely denominational in its outlook, it is deeply evangelical and catholic. That itself is one of the strongest and most persistent characteristics of the Kirk which should commend itself to readers from many other Churches. How happy we are that Dr Bulloch should have undertaken this task for us, to interpret the Church of Scotland to readers of The Christian Denominations Series.

Thomas F. Torrance
Moderator of the General Assembly

1

A National Church

One of the things that may surprise you if you go to America is the strength of the Baptist Church, especially in the south. In Britain Baptist churches are in a minority and their congregations are usually small though very loyal. But in Virginia and Carolina and many other southern states the Baptist churches are numerous, large, and handsome, and their congregations are enormous. Something not unlike this is found in the U.S.S.R.: outside the Orthodox Church, the Baptists are probably the strongest branch of the Christian Church in Russia. Many visitors have commented on the packed congregation of the Baptist Church in Moscow. This tells you that the Baptist Church in Britain is only part of a world wide fellowship. The Baptists are international, and so are most Churches.

But the very name of the Church of Scotland, like that of the Church of England, tells you that whatever world-wide contacts it may have, it is based on one country and on one part of the British Isles. The national Church of Scotland is Protestant, not Roman Catholic. It is not governed by bishops, like the

Church of England; it is Presbyterian, i.e. organised on democratic lines. If you live in Scotland and want to see what the Church of Scotland is like you will not have to go far. It has congregations in every part of the land. To maintain ministers and churches in outlying and thinly inhabited parts of Scotland, in the Orkney or Shetland Islands or the glens of the West Highlands, is far from easy but, since it is the national Church, the Church of Scotland provides them. If you live in a Scottish city or country town, you cannot be more than a few streets away from one of its churches. Even in each of the great new housing areas you will find a congregation of the Church of Scotland. In a country district or a country town the church building may be ancient or simply old-fashioned; in a new suburb it may be so modern that you hardly recognise it as a church; but everywhere in Scotland you will be within reach of a congregation of the Church of Scotland.

What is more, you will be living within one of her parishes. Whether its people remember the fact or not, every congregation of the Church of Scotland north of the English border is a parish church. A parish is an extent of land assigned to one church. In that district the parish church is responsible for setting the Christian faith before everyone who lives within its bounds. Some congregations forget this. Many have great problems in doing it. But the duty is there.

However, if you live outside Scotland you may have to go far to see a Church of Scotland congregation. Two large and historic congregations have been founded by Scots who have gone to live in London. Unexpectedly, there are two more at Corby in Lincolnshire. This is because many Scots went south when steelworks were transferred to Corby from the Clyde valley. A few other Scots 'kirks' are scattered throughout England.

English visitors often ask why in Scotland a church is called a kirk. The answer is that the words church and kirk are both derived from a Greek word used in the early Church and that the Scottish form, like the Dutch and German forms, happens to be a little closer to the original than is the English word 'church'.

Scots who emigrated to the former colonies founded their own kirks, but with time these tend to merge with the local Church as the older generation dies out and contact with Scotland grows less. At Calcutta the Scots kirk always had Indian members. Today it has an Indian minister and is part of the Church of North India.

In Europe congregations keep their connection with Scotland but also draw members from many nations. One example of this is at Geneva. There the congregation has a nucleus of Scots but other members are drawn from as far away as America, Scandinavia, Australia, and Japan. This Scots kirk gives substantial help to the struggling Spanish and Italian Protestant congregations in Geneva, and co-operates with the English-speaking Roman Catholic congregation in overseas aid. A casual visitor at Christmas, a Philippino missionary, was surprised to hear that the offering was going to Papua, from where she had just come.

We should not give the impression that the Church of Scotland is narrowly Scottish. Since it is Presbyterian it is part of the wider fellowship of many Churches in the tradition of the Reformation. Others in this tradition are the United Reformed Church in England and Wales, the Presbyterian Church in Ireland, and the Reformed Churches on the continent from Spain to Czechoslovakia, Hungary, and Poland. Nor has the Church of Scotland seen itself as sectarian. Without disrespect or ill will to other branches of the Christian Church in Scotland, it has traditionally regarded itself merely as the Catholic or 'Universal' Church in one country.

In other words, the Church of Scotland is simply a part of the one Christian Church as it is found in that one country and with something of a Scottish accent.

This means that the Church of Scotland depends upon those remarkable events in Palestine to which the whole Christian Church owes its existence. It depends on the fact that a small and obscure nation of the Middle East came to believe that all things in the universe owed their existence to one invisible God, that He demanded obedience to the moral law, and that He had a purpose of love for the whole world. Most of all, it draws its inspiration from the life, death, and resurrection of Jesus Christ, the community which He founded, and the record of these things in the New Testament. Through the centuries all this has been so closely interwoven with the life of Scotland that it has given the Church of Scotland something of a Scottish flavour. But this is to be expected. The Roman Catholic Church in Ireland and the Roman Catholic Church in Poland are all one Church, yet they are, in a sense, national churches too.

How far does the Church of Scotland represent Scotland today? Until the middle of the eighteenth century it came close to doing so completely. Three things ended this. The first was the arrival of many more Roman Catholics. In 1755 there were only five in the whole of the Clyde Valley but about 1790 many Roman Catholics came to Glasgow to work in the new factories, some from the Highlands but far more from Ireland. After the Irish potato famine, immigration increased, and in the autumn of 1973 the number of children entering Roman Catholic primary schools in Glasgow for the first time exceeded 50% of the total intake for the city. Secondly, there were divisions in the Church of Scotland, at first on a small scale but then on a large scale. Thirdly, and perhaps most important of all, the drastic social changes of the industrial revolution removed thousands from any active contact with the Church. Towns like Airdrie and Coatbridge sprang up in what had been sparse country parishes. Glasgow was scarcely more than a big village until about 1740. In that year it had less than 150 weddings, but in 1790 it had 1449. One Glasgow parish, that of the Barony Kirk, had 70 000 parishioners. No minister could cope with such numbers. The Church could not catch up with this growth.

There had always been those who did not believe the Christian faith and many who had little interest in it, but now there were many totally untouched by it. Thousands became pagan in fact if not in name. Yet there were many more churches, for in the nineteenth century Scotland had more Christian sects, or divisions, than ever before. There was much rivalry between different Churches and little co-operation. Too many churches were built in the wrong places. In small towns, which needed only one, there were usually three rival Presbyterian churches. In larger towns this was also true, but not so obvious. As a result a false impression was created. It is often thought that in Victorian Scotland everybody went to church and was strict in morals. This is not true. In 1837 a government commission reported that well over half the population of Edinburgh took no part in the Church. In Glasgow the proportion was higher still. Church attendance was almost unknown among the poor. As for morals, one child in every ten in Victorian Scotland was born outside marriage, and in the farming counties one child in six. The idea that, compared with Victorian times, ours is a permissive society, is an illusion.

What alienated thousands from the Church was not so much active disbelief as the nature of the society in which they lived after the industrial revolution. The Church was not blind to these grim facts. Men like Norman MacLeod of the Barony Kirk in Glasgow toiled among the poor. William Quarrier, a Baptist layman, founded the Orphan Homes of Scotland at Bridge of Weir on the principle of seeking no contributions except by prayer. James Begg, an Edinburgh Free Church minister, ran a co-operative building society which enabled working people to buy their own homes by instalments at a total cost of £180.

Other men set out to end divisions within the Church. Several small bodies had already come together. In 1900 the Free Church and the United Presbyterian Church joined to form the United Free Church and in 1929 the United Free Church and the Church of Scotland were united. There are still some small Presbyterian Churches in Scotland outside the Church of Scotland. Minorities of the Free Church and of the United Free Church refused to join the unions of 1900 and 1929. The Free Church is strong in parts of the Highlands but over most of the country the visitor would hardly be aware that these small Churches existed.

None of the other Presbyterian Churches in Scotland are as large as the Church of Scotland, and the Roman Catholic Church is the second largest Church in modern Scotland. Roughly one person in every five in Scotland today is a communicant member of the Church of Scotland. This figure is misleading in several ways. It is true that not all communicants are active members. On the other hand, since in Scotland people do not usually become communicants until their late teens this leaves all young people out of account. Even more important is the fact that there are very large numbers not on church rolls who would class themselves as Christian believers and would count themselves as attached to the Church of Scotland even if they give it very little active support. The divisions which once marked Protestant church life in Scotland have now almost disappeared. Even where some remain there is a new spirit of friendship and co-operation.

Think about . . .

Is a national Church in keeping with the New Testament idea of a Church?

Is there a place in the modern world for a national Church?

2

Its
Faith

Some branches of the Christian Church define very strictly the doctrines which they hold. For a long time the Scottish Church did so, but this is no longer the case. Anyone coming from a Church with strict doctrinal teaching may get the impression that the Church of Scotland has very little definite belief. But you must not be misled. In fact it lives by the Christian faith as it has been held since New Testament times, but it permits a great deal of liberty of opinion to its ministers and members. This is essential for any living community in an age of debate like our own – and it is true of more Churches than is often supposed.

When a child is baptised in the Scottish Church the father is asked if he holds the Christian faith. Sometimes the Apostles' Creed is used to define the faith, but more often the father is asked, 'In presenting your child for baptism, do you confess your faith in God as your heavenly Father, in Jesus Christ as your Saviour and Lord, and in the Holy Spirit as your Sanctifier?' The same words are used when an adult is baptised and when a candidate is being confirmed or – to use the phrase more commonly used in Scotland – admitted to full communion. Thus Christian conviction is combined with a great deal of freedom.

The creeds in which the early Church declared its faith are short. They deal with some of the central teaching of the Bible, and of the New Testament in particular. Later, in time of dispute, various branches of the Church drew up 'confessions' to express their own distinctive views. These differ from the creeds in being lengthy statements of doctrine. In 1560 the laymen who sat in the Scottish Parliament set out to make Scotland a Protestant country, but they had neither the knowledge nor the inclination for a theological debate, so they asked their ministers to write down an account of what they believed. Six of them, led by John Knox, were given the task and in a few days they produced what is known as *The Scots Confession*.

This was passed as an Act of Parliament. Written in a hurry and in the heat of controversy, it had a flavour which the modern reader will think to be strongly anti-Roman. Like most war-time writing it lacked charity and tolerance, but by the standards of that troubled age it was surprisingly mild. *The Catholic Encyclopaedia* generously says that it was 'written in a vigorous, original and, for a document proceeding from the pen of Knox, in an extremely moderate style.' On the whole it is a simple, straightforward statement of the Christian faith. The men who drafted it intended to write nothing in it but what was warranted by the Bible. They had no thought of writing a new faith. Nor did they mean to displace the creeds, and at the time they used the Apostles' Creed in baptism and Sunday worship and expected communicants to be able to say it. Their intention was to state the orthodox Catholic doctrine as it continued to be believed in the Reformed Church and to exclude any corruptions.

During the civil wars of the seventeenth century or, as we would say in Scotland, in the time of the Covenanters, the Church of Scotland accepted *The Westminster Confession*. This had been drawn up in 1643 in the vain hope that it would be accepted by all the Churches in Great Britain and Ireland; in the end it was only the Presbyterians, including the Church of

Scotland, that did so. *The Westminster Confession* is an even longer document than *The Scots Confession*. Ever since 1647 it has been, after the Bible, the chief statement of the faith of the Church of Scotland. For years the Church tried to make all its people familiar with the teaching of the Confession, by using two catechisms (lists of questions and answers) – the *Larger Catechism* for use by preachers and the *Shorter Catechism* for the training of children. Today *The Westminster Confession* is not much studied. It is written in old-fashioned language and it reflects too much the bitter religious differences of Cromwell's time.

Several attempts have been made to write a statement of the Christian faith as it is held in the Scottish Church today, but it cannot be said that they have been very successful. The most recent was *A Short Statement of the Church's Faith*, published in 1935. What is written in the next few paragraphs is based upon it, but it is astonishing how old fashioned even the language of this document seems today, and another fresh statement is now being written by a committee.

1. Since the time of Christ the Church and the Bible have both set the faith before men, but the Scottish Church holds that the Church can be at fault and at times has been, while the Bible remains unchanged and therefore must be the supreme authority in its testimony to Christ. The Bible is the guide to what Christians must believe about God, about Jesus Christ, and the meaning of human life. This conviction lay at the root of the great division of the Church at the time of the Reformation. Later disputes between Roman Catholics and Protestants sometimes made the division even greater, and there are still some extremists on both sides. However, if the Scottish Reformers had known the Roman Catholic Church as it is today, since the Second Vatican Council, it is doubtful if they would have thought of breaking away from it.

The belief that the Bible is the chief guide for Christians does not mean that it is a textbook of science or history, but that it has the power to lead the reader to timeless truths about God and the deeper meaning of life. When the Spirit of God is working in his mind, Christians say, the reader can hear the Word of God speaking to him through these pages. That is why Protestant Christians believe it should be available to all. It was a Scottish professor, James Moffat, who produced the first notable modern translation of the Bible, and it was in the Church of Scotland that the proposals were first made which resulted in the production of *The New English Bible*.

2. But more important than creeds or confessions, more important even than the Bible, is the person of Jesus Christ. The Scottish *Shorter Catechism* begins with a very deep question:

'What is the chief end of man?' (i.e. what is the purpose of our being here on earth?)

It replies:

'Man's chief end is to glorify God and to enjoy Him for ever.'

God may be known in many ways, and at many times and places. But for Christians He is known fully only in Jesus Christ.

Christians speak of God as Father, Son and Holy Spirit, but He is still one God. He is holy, righteous, and wise, but the heart of the Christian faith is the conviction that God is love. His love was shown to men in Jesus Christ. All the fullness of God was present in Christ, but He humbled Himself, accepted the limitations of manhood, and came to live a life among us as one of us. In obedience to the will of His Father and in love for men Jesus suffered death, but God raised Him from the dead and He is now Lord of all. Christ revealed God to men as no other has done and it is He alone Who brings men to God.

3. We believe that God created man as part of the world of nature but with this difference – He made him a spiritual being with the image of God upon him, with an enquiring mind and a capacity for creativity. Yet man went astray. Evil entered his life. Because of this men are alienated from God even though in one sense they are also drawn to Him. Despite all the gifts with which they are endowed something always goes wrong with men's lives until they receive God's forgiveness and His grace in Christ. Those who follow Christ are called to live in fellowship with God and in love with one another, to take a part in the worship and prayer of the Church, to serve God's kingdom among men,

17

and to live for the service of God and of others, in this life and hereafter.

4. We believe that the Catholic or Universal Church is greater than any denomination of Christians. It is the fellowship of all who confess Christ and of their children.

If you belong to another branch of the Christian Church you may find that some of the forms of worship and organisation in the Church of Scotland are unfamiliar to you, but you are unlikely to find much that is novel in what its people believe. Differences which once may have seemed important are slipping away in the modern world.

If you do not come from another branch of the Church you will find the faith of the Church of Scotland not merely in the way it is preached on Sundays but even more in the way in which it is lived in believing families and households. We do not suppose that practising Christians automatically live a faultless life. Anyone who reads the New Testament will know that Christ said that He came 'not to call the righteous, but sinners to repentance.' Yet there is a strong conviction among Scots that the first obligation of a Christian is Christian conduct, and especially towards one's neighbour. It is felt to be a disgrace to a minister or member if he shows a lack of true charity. While the Church teaches that God asks much more from a man, it is noticeable that it is almost unknown for active members of the Church to commit offences which will bring conviction in a criminal court. The writer once knew a church member who was sentenced for petty theft. He never returned to church. This shows that he misunderstood, and probably his neighbours too, what the Christian faith is about, but it also shows the strength of the expectation that a church member will be upright and keep the moral law in his work and his marriage. Love is more important than the law, and it will be found, in Church of Scotland circles, that love is not lacking.

Think about . . .

How are faith and conduct related?

Should members of the same church hold exactly the same doctrine?

Do you find anything in the beliefs of the Church of Scotland that you do not find in other branches of the Christian Church? If not, why do the various branches remain separate?

3

Its
Worship

If you live in Scotland and go down to Lincolnshire
or East Anglia you will be surprised to find that even
the smallest village has a magnificent mediaeval church,
often far too large for the population. We never had
as many great churches in the North because Scotland
was a poorer country in the Middle Ages. Most Scots
now live in the industrial towns which grew up in the
nineteenth century. Lots of them suppose that all
Scottish churches are like those in their own neigh-
bourhood. They are mistaken, for in Scotland there
are many types of church buildings.

MEDIAEVAL CHURCHES   If you want to see an example
of a Norman church dating from the twelfth century
you can see one at Dalmeny about twelve miles west
of Edinburgh. There is another at Leuchars near
St Andrews. Each is built on simple lines with heavy
masonry and deep carving at the arches. Far to the
north, at Kirkwall in the Orkneys, is a great Norman
cathedral built very soon after Dalmeny and Leuchars.
Glasgow Cathedral, dating mostly from the thirteenth
century, is the most complete mediaeval cathedral in

Scotland today. It once had two west towers, which now are missing, but otherwise it is complete. The western half, which is called the nave, is separated from the eastern half, the choir, by a heavy stone screen; during the Middle Ages the nave was the only part normally open to laymen. The choir was for the clergy, of whom there were many. This cathedral was built on a sloping site so that it could be above the burial place of St Mungo, the first bishop. It was therefore necessary to build a lower church, or crypt, under the choir. After the Reformation the use of the whole building was something of a problem, as it would be today in any branch of the Church. At one time it was divided into three churches. Today the congregation worships in the choir and the nave is used only when the building is crowded on public occasions.

The most famous church in Scotland, St Giles in the High Street of Edinburgh, is deceptive. Though it is full of history it was only a cathedral for a short time in the seventeenth century. Originally it was a parish church which grew in size as chapels were added to it. Late in the Middle Ages St Michael's Church was built in Linlithgow and St John's in Perth. These are among the few Scottish churches that can compare with the great parish churches of England. The average parish church in mediaeval Scotland was a simple oblong, some twenty feet wide and forty to ninety feet long, depending on the numbers in the parish.

NINETEENTH CENTURY CHURCHES   However, most Scots are not accustomed to these ancient churches. In the nineteenth century towns grew larger, and new churches were built; the commonest type, whatever it was made to look like outside, was a large oblong, with a gallery, and a pulpit in the middle of one wall. Later the pattern changed again. Churches were designed to emphasise the place of the sacraments in worship, so the communion table was placed at the end of the main aisle of the church, and the pulpit placed to one side; the sermon was made less important than the communion. There were also two side-aisles separated by pillars.

Another point should be noticed. The old-fashioned country church stood in the middle of a churchyard. The new town churches stood in streets and they did not stand alone; each had halls attached to it for the weekday activities of the congregation. Organisations for young people, such as Girl Guides, Boys Brigade, and Boy Scouts, Guilds for adult members, Kirk Sessions and committees carried on their work here.

MODERN CHURCHES When the second world war ended vast numbers of new houses were needed and the resources of the Church were strained to keep pace with them. Since then the Church of Scotland has built over two hundred and forty churches. At first dual-purpose buildings called hall churches were erected, with a communion table and pulpit at one end for Sunday worship. During the week this could be screened off and the seating turned towards the other end where there was a platform or stage. Only financial pressure caused this expedient, and these buildings have proved very unsatisfactory.

A new church: St Ninian's.

So once again churches were built with a hall close by. Sometimes the manse – the house for the minister – was built in the same complex of buildings. This was not a return to the traditional style of building: modern churches like St Ninian's in the new town of Glenrothes in Fife, opened in 1972, would scarcely be recognised by our grandparents as churches if they could see them. There was a time when Scottish churches had a long communion table with the pulpit behind it. At communion the congregation sat around the table and the bread and wine were passed from hand to hand as must have been done at the last supper of our Lord. Since 1950 there has been a return to this pattern of the central communion table, not only in the Scottish Church but in buildings such as the new Roman Catholic cathedrals at Liverpool and Clifton. The minister is seen as one of the worshipping congregation and not contrasted with them as in a Victorian church.

CHURCH SERVICES   As there are differences in church buildings so there are differences in the way in which services are conducted. Worship in the Church of England is shaped by the Prayer Book and in the Roman Catholic Church by the Missal. In Scotland *The Book of Common Order* is available to the minister as an example, but there is no obligation for him to follow it exactly. In ordinary Sunday worship few ministers do so. They conduct the service in their own words but more or less on the same lines.

Most Scottish churches have their main service at 11 o'clock on a Sunday morning, or round about that time. Quite a number hold an evening service as well, but generally these have always been poorly attended. Where there are strong congregations two morning services are held – a custom fairly common in America.

A service usually opens with a psalm or hymn. The minister then calls on the people to join in prayer. Scottish people, for the most part, sit when they pray and bow their heads. In the first prayer we usually ask God's presence and His aid in our worship, we confess our sins together, and ask for God's pardon and for His help in the Christian life. Then come readings ('lessons') from the Old and New Testaments. *The Book of Common Order* expects that the Apostles' Creed will be said by all after the New Testament lesson, but comparatively few churches do so today. A second prayer contains thanksgiving for all God's goodness to us and intercessions for the Church and the world of men. At intervals between the lessons and prayers hymns are sung. Then comes the sermon; though it has a personal character it is not meant to be an account of the minister's own opinions but the proclamation of the message of the Bible. A lot of importance – possibly too much importance – has been placed on the sermon in Scotland. Gifts of money (the 'offering') are received and dedicated for the service of God. There is a short prayer of dedication, a hymn is sung, and the service closes with the blessing. Scottish services were once notoriously lengthy, but it is unusual now for a service to last more than an hour. People nowadays would find it difficult to attend to the very long sermons which were once preached.

The Scottish Church has always taught that it is the duty and privilege of its people to join in worship each Lord's Day, but it must be admitted that only a minority do so regularly and that the average member comes to worship occasionally. The conditions of modern life have encouraged this. Where industry works round the clock on a shift basis even the most loyal office-bearers often find themselves working on Sundays. At one time in Scotland Sunday was observed more strictly than in England or on the continent. Games on Sunday were frowned on. Mass communications such as television have changed this except in some parts of the northern Highlands.

Scholars who study Christian worship point out that worship in Scotland today differs from the intention of the Reformers, and the practice of some other branches of the Church, in leaving too much to the minister and too little part in worship to others. Whatever the reason may be, Scottish congregations today seem reluctant to join audibly in prayer.

Now let us look at some other acts of worship. The Scottish Church celebrates acts of worship such as ordination, confirmation, and marriage, but does not describe them as sacraments as some other Churches do. The reason for this lies in the way we define a sacrament and not in the value placed upon it. Christ did not command all His followers to be married or ordained, but He did command them to be baptised and to take part in the communion. It is because of this that the Church of Scotland reserves the name of sacrament for these two. In each case the most important matters, the elements used and the words spoken, are given to us in the New Testament.

BAPTISM   We believe that baptism should take place in the presence of the congregation since it is an act, not of the minister alone, but of the whole Church. Different Presbyterian Churches have now united in the Church of Scotland and their practice in baptism has not always been uniform. In an old parish church it was almost unknown for a minister to refuse baptism to any child. In other congregations children were not baptised unless at least one of the parents, and preferably both, were active members of the congregation who showed signs of fulfilling the promises which they made. For some time there was also serious debate about whether the baptism of infants was fully justified, but the mind of the Church is that all children born into Christian homes should be baptised and so brought up in the membership of the Church.

When a child is baptised the parents stand before the font. First the minister reads the verses from the Gospel in which baptism is commanded by Christ. He then explains the meaning of what is being done and the obligations assumed by the parents. 'By this sacrament we are solemnly admitted into the membership of Christ's Church, and are engaged to be the Lord's.' This promise, he says, is made to our children also since they are being brought into the family and household of faith. Next he reads the verses which tell how Jesus received the children when His disciples turned them away. The father of the child is then asked if he holds the Christian faith. There is a short prayer. The minister then takes the child from the arms of the father, names him or her, and says, 'I baptise thee in the name of the Father, and of the Son, and of the Holy Spirit.' The congregation joins

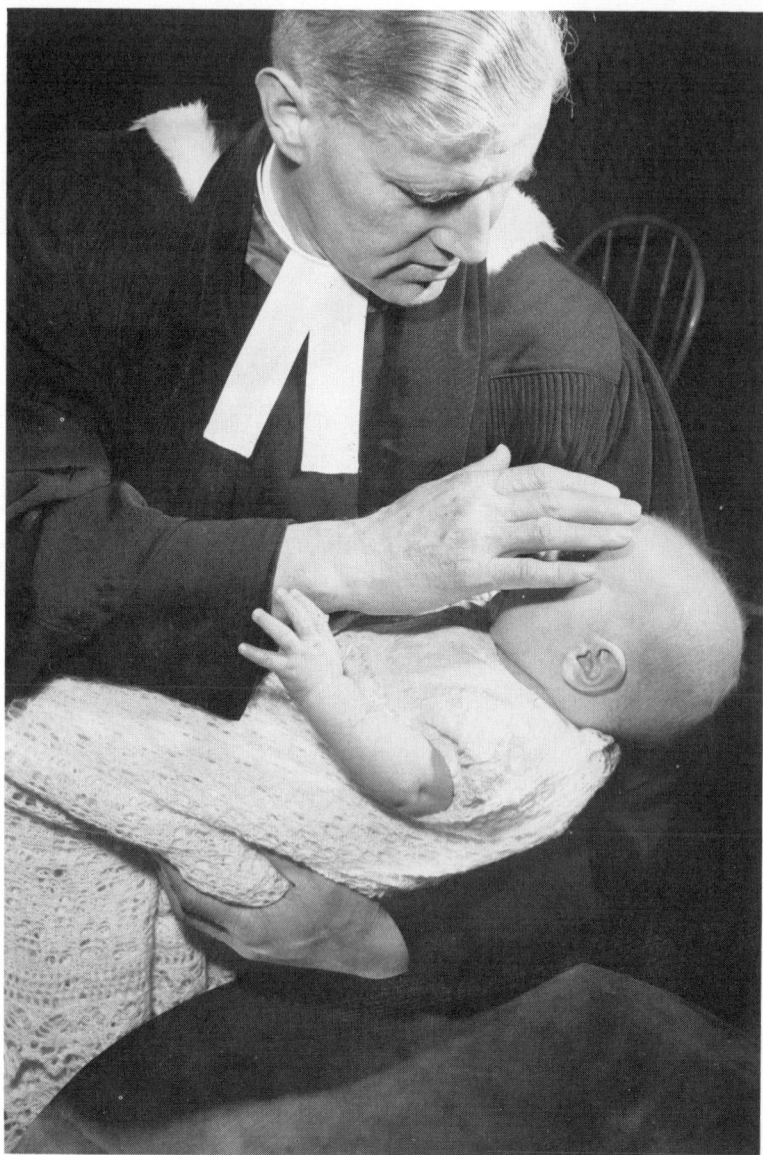

Baptism.

in a blessing. The child is declared to be admitted, not into the Church of Scotland, but 'into the membership of the holy Catholic Church.'

We have described here the baptism of a baby. The baptism of an adult is much the same except that in this case, of course, the questions are put directly to the person who is to be baptised. It is often forgotten that about 1500 adults are baptised every year in the Church of Scotland, some because their parents for some reason or other neglected to have them baptised, but most of them because their parents were not believers and they are coming into the Christian Church for the first time. At least one minister of the Scottish Church was baptised in this way when he became a Christian believer. The writer of this once conducted a service where thirteen adults were baptised together.

COMMUNION Though a child is a member of the Church from the time of baptism he has not been able to make that personal confession which is essential for a Christian. When he is old enough to make his own decision, has faced all the questions which ought to rise in our minds, and has decided that he believes in Christ as his Lord, he becomes a communicant. This is sometimes known in Scotland as 'confirmation' but more commonly as 'admission to the Lord's Supper'. Those who are admitted stand before the congregation. The minister tells how they were baptised and have now come to confirm the 'covenant' (sacred agreement) then made on their behalf. They are called on to declare that they hold the Christian faith, to promise to live in dependence on God, and to share in all ways in the life of the Church. Usually the minister then lays his hand on the head of each, prays that they may be confirmed in the faith, and admits them to the Lord's Table.

Before the Reformation the laity received communion only at long intervals and often only at Easter. The Reformers were anxious to have a weekly celebration, but long-standing custom prevailed and communion in Scotland has traditionally been celebrated only occasionally. In some congregations it is only celebrated twice yearly, and in most about four times. You may also find that your local church is beginning to hold a communion service at Christmas and Easter, whereas fifty years ago practically no Scottish churches held services on Christmas Day or Good Friday.

We said that *The Book of Common Order* is seldom followed exactly at a service in most churches. It seems, however, that it is much more often followed at a communion service, though there is growing complaint that its language is old-fashioned. On a Communion Sunday the service follows the pattern of an ordinary service except that the Nicene Creed is included. After the sermon the minister goes to the communion table and is joined by the elders, if they are not already there. Using the words of Jesus, he invites the people to join in the sacrament. A psalm or hymn is sung. On the table, which is covered with a white cloth, are set the bread and communion cups. The bread and wine are offered to God. The minister says, 'The grace of the Lord Jesus Christ be with you all.' He next reads what is called the warrant, the passage in which St Paul tells how our Lord instituted the sacrament. He takes the bread and wine and sets them apart from all common use. Next comes the communion prayer, an act of thanksgiving to God, of remembrance of the death of Christ, and of dedication. The minister takes the bread, breaks it, and speaks the words of our Lord, 'Take, eat, this is My body, which is broken for you. This do in remembrance of Me.' He then takes the cup, raises it, and says, 'This cup is the new covenant in My blood; this do ye, as oft as ye drink it, in remembrance of Me.' A short prayer follows. The minister takes the bread and wine himself. As he hands the bread to the elders he says, 'Take ye, eat ye; this is the body of Christ which is broken for you; this do in remembrance of Him.' Next, giving the cup, he says, 'This cup is the new covenant in the blood of Christ, which is shed for many unto remission of sins; drink ye all of it.' At this point the elders take the bread and wine to the communicants. There is silence; for those present are not merely remembering Christ but receiving Him into their lives. When all have received, and the bread and wine are replaced on the table and covered, the minister says, 'The peace

A communion service.

of the Lord Jesus Christ be with you all.' There follows a short prayer in which we remember those we love who have died in the faith, a psalm is sung, and the service closes with the blessing.

MARRIAGE   Another act of worship – the marriage service – is of importance to most people. In this matter Scots law has long differed from English law. Once upon a time when young lovers could not get married in England they eloped across the Border to get married by the blacksmith at Gretna Green. Behind this lay the fact that the law of Scotland regarded marriage as a binding contract into which a man and woman entered by mutual consent. The writer once knew a couple who had seven children but had never had any wedding ceremony. Yet, if it had been questioned, there could have been no doubt that they were legally married, for all their neighbours and friends could testify that the two had lived together and had always spoken of each other as man and wife. However, the law has now been changed. The marriage contract, like any other contract, has sometimes to be proved, and it is not always so easily proved as in this case. Marriages by simple agreement, whether at Gretna Green or anywhere else, were liable to abuse. So the law has now been altered, as the Church of Scotland long wished, and today if you are to be married in Scotland there must be either a religious service or a civil wedding at a registrar's office.

Marriage is more than a private affair, so the intention to be married must be made public, either by the calling of banns in church or by a notice in a registrar's window. A wedding in church is not just a matter of a white dress and many guests; it is a decision by the bride and groom to enter their married life in the Christian faith and to keep their promises throughout life in dependence on God's help. A wedding can take place in church, and often does, with no more present than the bride and groom, two witnesses, and the minister. When it takes place with more present the service usually opens with a hymn. Otherwise it begins with the minister declaring the nature of Christian marriage, and then calling for anyone who knows any legal

objection to this marriage to speak. After a prayer the bride and groom exchange vows, a ring is given and received, and the two are declared to be husband and wife and blessed. Some verses from the New Testament are read and the wedding ends with a prayer and the benediction.

It may be thought that we have spent a lot of time describing the worship of the Church of Scotland. But what people do is often more significant than what they say. Worship is one of the things the Church does. It tells you that its members live in reliance on God and find the meaning of life in the Christian faith. There are, of course, many other things the Church does which can, or should, be seen in daily life, at home and at work.

Think about . . .

Have you visited churches other than your local one? Why do some churches, both in the Church of Scotland and the Roman Catholic Church, have the communion table or altar in the centre of the church? Does this indicate a change in attitudes?

Are your local church services like those in *The Book of Common Order*?

4

Inside a Congregation

A Church is like a political party or any other society with ideals. The outsider does not know 'what makes it tick'. He never quite understands what it means to the people within it. It is fully understood only from within, and in the Scottish Church this means from within a congregation. In this chapter let us imagine what it would be like to belong to a congregation. Unfortunately, there is no such thing as an average congregation. Some are in lonely places, others in cities; some are small and intimate, others are large and not so intimate as they should be. So let us choose a congregation which is very much part of the modern world.

Once upon a time Holy Trinity Church stood in the centre of Edinburgh until its ancient building was swept away to make room for the shunting yards of Waverley Railway Station. It was rebuilt, as nearly as possible, and still in the heart of the city where today there are few residents but many clearances and office blocks. The time had come when it was obvious that a church in this decaying and over-churched part of the city had no useful future, so in 1969 it was decided to transfer it once again. This time it was transferred to Wester Hailes, several miles out from the city centre.

In 1969 there were no houses at Wester Hailes and only green fields, but Edinburgh Corporation had marked it out for a housing scheme. Two years passed before a house was built. Meantime the minister and congregation continued in the old church, but as houses started to go up work was increasingly diverted to the new parish. Only a handful of houses were of the bungalow or cottage type. Scottish townsfolk have always lived in flats, and modern conditions demand it. But high-rise flats of twenty-five or thirty storeys have been found to have unexpected problems, so none of the flats in Wester Hailes are in blocks of more than nine storeys. Edinburgh had need of houses for elderly people, so slightly over a quarter of the new homes had only two apartments (two rooms).

The vital statistics of a parish like Wester Hailes are quite frightening. The population is about 20 000: no exact figures are available. There are about 5000 houses. Many residents are elderly. A fair proportion of others are single parent families and unmarried mothers. 'Comparable in fact with the size of many new towns,' said its minister, as he began to explain some of the challenges facing this kirk and the problems created for the residents in an area this size. 'Wester Hailes is a high amenity scheme in which even a modest two-apartment house can cost up to £5 a week to heat and light and quite a number of people cannot cope with expensive rents and running costs.' It is not a scheme built for one class of the community. A few wealthy families may be found, but there are all sorts of families including those living on social security payments. So mixed a district does not easily form an integrated community where people all know one another.

'What is more of a problem, however, and one which presents a direct challenge to the kirk, is the boredom and isolation, particularly among housewives and those confined indoors.' This has sometimes been called New Town Sickness. About a third of the houses are of three apartments and designed for young married couples. If their families grow they are liable to move to bigger houses. Residents come and go; there is a rapid turnover; and newcomers can often remain strangers and lonely for a long time.

Before Christmas 1972 a new church and halls had been put up at a cost of about £92 000. If you were to join the Church of Scotland in Wester Hailes this would be your kirk. A new congregation, as this virtually is, however old it may be in name, has not the slightest chance of paying a bill of £92 000, or of staffing the buildings adequately. The price obtained for the former church when it was abandoned went towards paying for the new one. Otherwise the cost was met by a committee of the Church of Scotland, and as it gathers strength it is expected that the new congregation will gradually repay a share of the sum. When the change was made from the old building all but a handful of the old congregation dropped off and went to churches nearer their homes, while a new membership came in, as was hoped, from round about. As to the precise number, 'I haven't a clue,' says the minister. At any rate it passed 500 some time ago and is rapidly growing.

Old-fashioned country congregations once drew all their financial support from endowments (money left by wealthy supporters in days gone by). They still draw something from these, but town congregations generally depend entirely on the givings of their members. A congregational board of elected members is responsible for finance. It has to pay the staff, maintain the buildings, heat and light them, and give to Christian charity and the wider work of the Church.

The Church of Scotland is not paid for by the government, but it is a national church and closely related to the community around it. At Wester Hailes the congregation runs the usual activities such as Sunday School and Bible Class, Guides, Scouts and Boys' Brigade, as well as organisations for older people. Three primary schools have been built and a fourth is planned; there is also a secondary school, but a new suburb like Wester Hailes lacks much that would exist in an older district. A shopping centre has recently been opened, but as yet there is no full scale community centre, except for some accommodation in schools. So the kirk co-operates to some degree with the welfare activities of local government. It runs an old folks' club and a lunch club for the elderly. In co-operation with the Edinburgh Education Department it runs a nursery class and there have been other classes on subjects from dressmaking to yoga.

Leading the congregation is a minister who, in this case, has to be young and active. He has an assistant minister, who is likely to change each year, a deaconess responsible for work among women and children, and a youth worker. But no Presbyterian Church expects to be run only by its paid staff: its success depends on the amount of work and service given by committed members. Like every Scottish church Wester Hailes has a kirk session. Until recently the elders who compose it had to be men, but now women can become both ministers and elders. The Session represents the congregation and also cares for it and supervises it. Each elder has a district of his own where he is expected to visit and get to know all the church members in it. Living in the same streets are many who are not members of any congregation. If these are to get to know what the Church means, it must be through the example and influence of the church members living among them. At communion times the elder issues a card to each member. This is used to record attendance, so that it can be known how far individual members are taking some part in the life of the congregation. Done in spare time after work, the task of eldership is demanding and calls for conviction. Something is wrong if a Scotttish church depends on its ministers too much. A strong and active kirk session (meeting of elders) contributes at least as much to its welfare as any minister.

The Young Wives and Mothers Group joins with the Guild of Service to conduct a social club for unsupported parents. It is safe to say that, at Wester Hailes, this type of congregation will keep on growing in many ways.

Let us now look at a rather different congregation. In 1963, when the new industrial town of Livingston was about to be built in a rural part of Scotland between Glasgow and Edinburgh, an appeal was made to the Church to start something entirely new at Livingston and not be content with the familiar pattern. As a result there was an agreement between the Church of Scotland, the Scottish Episcopal Church, and the Scottish Congregational Union to make Livingston an experimental 'ecumenical' area, that is to say, an area in which the Churches work, not separately, but together. In October 1968 the Methodist Church in Scotland also joined the experiment.

In January 1966 Brian Hardy, an Episcopal minister, and James Maitland from the Church of Scotland, were inducted together, by Bishop and Presbytery, for the first time functioning together. As yet there were no buildings. People began to arrive in April, 1966, so that in this case the Church was here to welcome the people. It was very much a part of the new community, helping to shape it, and give some sense of purpose and well-being. Out of its initiatives came the New Town Forum, a kind of local parliament, whose job it was to get something done, by the people rather than the authorities, about the snags and growing pains encountered in the early years. There was an endeavour to meet people as they came to live in the New Town, but stress was laid not so much on first contacts as forming and developing good neighbourly relationships. This work was entrusted to counsellors, visitors and church members themselves.

Until October 1969 Riverside Primary School was used for worship and meetings, but then St. Columba's church was opened. This had been paid for by the Church of Scotland. A second church, St. Paul's, was built by the Episcopal Church in Scotland in 1971. A third is now being built by the Scottish Congregational Union. Here Roman Catholics and Protestants will be sharing the same place of worship though at different times. Serving this venture of faith is a ministry of six, two Episcopal priests, a Methodist deaconess, a Congregational minister, and two Church of Scotland ministers.

'Part of the gain as part of the pain of being in the Church in Livingston,' says James Maitland, its first minister from the Church of Scotland, 'is that you are not allowed to be a mere passenger, that you are called into active participation in the life and mission of God's people in this place. Many more gains could be listed, but perhaps the most important of all is the new openness towards the unchurched that is a direct consequence of our being opened up to each other as members together in one household of faith.'

These are examples of congregations in a contemporary setting, coping, or trying to cope, with the work of the Church in a changing society at a time when old divisions within the Church have ceased to count. At the same time the Scottish Church, with so long a history behind it, is burdened with too much organisation that belongs to the past. All the country congregations began their life at a time when men walked to church or, at the most, came on horseback. Today we live in the age of the motor car, and the number of people living and working on the land is only a fraction of what once it was. But the country churches are there, and their people are attached to them. They have loyalties and rights and, of course, prejudices, so the policy of the Church has been to support country churches but to unite several under the one minister. Similarly in small towns and city centres congregations have been united and superfluous church buildings closed as urban life has changed. In this way the Church has been able to provide ministers and buildings for new suburbs like Wester Hailes and new towns like Livingston. Since 1949, when it first was possible to build after the war, 241 new buildings have been opened. This is not just a matter of stone and lime. It means that new congregations have been founded, and, in almost all instances, have become strong and vigorous.

Think about . . .

Is a church building necessary for the life of a congregation?

Do families in new housing areas lose touch with the Church? Or do they meet it for the first time?

5

How Presbyterianism Works

The Church of Scotland is both Protestant and Presbyterian. There is a widespread impression that this has been so since the Reformation, but if the first part is true the second is only partly so. The Reformation began in Germany in 1517, and in England Henry VIII began his break with the papacy about 1531. In Scotland it did not come until 1560. If the Roman Church was weak in Scotland, so were the Protestants. Most critics of the Church would have been content with a redistribution of the wealth of the Church, married clergy, worship in English instead of Latin, and an end to the political power of the Bishops. How Scotland became Presbyterian is rather a complicated story.

At the beginning of the sixteenth century Scotland was a poor and backward country. Its great fear was that it would be overrun and dominated by England. When England became Protestant, under Henry VIII, Scotland strengthened its ties with Catholic France. King James V of Scotland, nephew of Henry VIII, married Mary of Lorraine, of the powerful French Catholic family of Guise. Their daughter was known as 'Mary, Queen of Scots'. When she grew up, Mary was engaged to marry Francis, heir to the throne of France. For safety, Mary was sent to France while her French mother, Mary of Guise, became regent of Scotland. Four years later, when Mary married Francis, it was plain that Scotland was now to become a province of France. There was even a secret agreement, signed by Mary, that if she were to die without heirs Scotland would go to France. This danger led all those who believed in Scottish independence to join forces with the Protestants, who until then had been regarded simply as allies of England. There were risings in many parts of Scotland. The regent, Mary of Guise, brought in more French troops to put down the rebellion. Matters went badly for the reformers, until help came from England. At length a treaty was signed between France and England: all French soldiers were withdrawn from Scotland, and Frenchmen were debarred from all important posts in its government.

In August 1560, the Scottish Parliament adopted Protestantism as the official creed of the realm. Mary and her husband, in France, refused to ratify this, and it did not become law until Mary abdicated seven years later, but the majority of the nation supported Parliament, so Knox and his associates went on to reorganise the Church on Protestant lines. They adopted a system worked out in the city of Geneva by John Calvin. In December, 1560, a meeting was held which is now regarded as the first Scottish 'General Assembly'. The following month they presented to Parliament their plans for the reorganisation of the Church. In each parish there should be a minister and elders holding office with the agreement of the congregation. The minister and elders would act as a disciplinary board. In the larger towns there would be meetings for discussion (the beginnings of 'presbyteries'). Over all was the General Assembly. With this reorganisation of the Church Knox had plans for national education and the relief of the poor. Knox believed that Church wealth should be used in three ways – to support the Church, for education, and to help the poor. Many in Parliament agreed, but it was opposed by the nobles, and the plan was not adopted. However, in a short time the Church was reorganised on

'Presbyterian' lines. In every parish a kirk session was formed and a General Assembly met annually to oversee the whole Church, but there were no presbyteries until 1581. Until now the Church had always been ruled by bishops and it took the Scottish Church some time to make up its mind about this. In the end the Church of Scotland, which had been relatively wealthy, became one of the poorest Churches in Europe.

John Knox had great gifts as an orator. He could sway crowds. He was a radical social and religious reformer, but he was also a dogmatic man who would not compromise or work with others. His colleagues came to regard him as an extremist and edged him out of the leadership. Nevertheless he had a strong power base among the ordinary people, at the grass roots of national life. He has remained one of the great figures of controversy in Scottish history. His character and influence have become something of a legend; and legends, we should remember, commonly contain a mixture of truth and fiction.

Knox stood closer to the working classes than many of his colleagues. As we saw, he had intended that the wealth of the Church should be retained and used, not only for its maintenance, but for a school in every parish, for the universities, and for a national system of poor relief. But the nobles, formerly poor, but now suddenly enriched, did not share his dream. Grudgingly, they permitted a share of the endowments for the support of the Church, much less for schools, and nothing for poor relief. The beginnings of Presbyterianism – the government of the Church by committees at congregational, district, and national levels – could be seen; but there were also bishops. Superintendents were appointed to carry out many of the functions of the bishops and two of the former bishops acted as superintendents. In the days before the Reformation the Scottish bishops had held great political power and had been instruments by which the crown held control of the country. The Scottish Protestants intended to put an end to this.

Today Presbyterianism is thought of only in terms of church life, but in an older Scotland it was also a political phenomenon, standing for local government by the people as opposed to centralised and authoritarian government. By its representative character it was planned to express public feeling from the popular level upwards until it determined national policy. Thus if it was Parliament which opposed Charles I in England it was the Kirk which opposed him in Scotland. It reflected the democratic element in Scottish life and it was this, and not manners or fashion, which Charles II had in mind when he said to Lauderdale that Presbyterianism was no religion for a gentleman. He associated it, correctly, with the voice of those beneath the rank of the landed gentry.

But this is to anticipate. When Queen Mary's son, James VI, came to power and commenced restoring the power of the crown he resented Presbyterianism. Gradually he reinstated the bishops in their former powers, not for religious but for political reasons. After he became King of England he restored the Scottish Episcopate in 1610. This might have been permanent if his son, Charles I, out of touch with Scottish opinion, had not determined to force a form of the English *Book of Common Prayer* on the Scottish Church by his own authority. He badly mismanaged his case, and the combined opposition roused almost all Scotland against him in the National Covenant of 1638. This was the start of the Civil Wars which cost him his throne and his life. The Covenanters have held a legendary position in popular Scottish history, but by the time of the restoration of the monarchy in 1660 they had so outrun public opinion that the nation at large accepted the return of the bishops with little protest.

By this time the remaining Covenanters were regarded as extremists by most Scots and once again the Episcopate might have remained but for events in England. James was deposed in 1688 and his successor, William of Orange, restored control of the Scottish Church to the Presbyterians with a warning that there should be no intolerance. Ever since then there have been no bishops in the Scottish Church; it has been Presbyterian.

Earlier we described how Presbyterianism works through a kirk session in a congregation and parish. The parish of Wester Hailes is on the outskirts of Edinburgh and so forms part of the

Presbytery of Edinburgh which is responsible for the oversight of the churches throughout the city. Each congregation sends its minister and one elder to sit and vote in the presbytery. Ministers and elders have equal rights and duties. With the new reorganisation of local government, presbyteries are having their boundaries redrawn so that they correspond to those of the new units of district government. There are also higher courts, formed by ministers and elders, called synods. These are planned to have the same bounds as the new regional authorities, but the synods play little part in Church life today. Three courts really matter, the kirk session at parish level, the presbytery at district level, and the General Assembly at national level.

Towards the end of May each year the General Assembly, the governing body of the Church of Scotland, meets in Edinburgh. It is a representative body. Many shades of opinion are found in its membership. Once in every four years each congregation sends its minister and an elder. They come from every part of Scotland and from every class of the community. A Gaelic speaker from the Western Isles may find himself next to an elder who is a worker in a car assembly plant. However, the gathering now has two main defects. Firstly, though women can now be members their numbers are still too few. This will right itself in time, but the second is more serious. The average member is too old, and this is harder to remedy since few younger men can afford to take a week off from their work.

The Moderator – the Assembly's chairman for the current year – takes his seat. Beneath him are the members of Assembly, some 1500 in number, and behind them the public gallery. The public gallery is open to anyone who can find space, and in recent years some schools have sent groups of pupils to listen to debates. Immediately behind the Moderator is a gallery for the Lord High Commissioner and his suite. The Lord High Commissioner is chosen by the government to represent the Queen. He or she is someone who has given notable public service. In 1970 the appointment was held by Miss Margaret Herbison, a miner's daughter, who had been a teacher in Allan Glen's School in Glasgow and later a Member of Parliament and cabinet minister.

While the Assembly meets the Lord High Commissioner lives in the Palace of Holyroodhouse and has the precedence given to the sovereign whom he (or, in Miss Herbison's case, she) represents. The only exception to this is when the Queen herself is present.

This element of pomp and ceremony should not be misunderstood. The Queen is not Head of the Church of Scotland. She or her deputy attends to show interest in the work of the Church, and to acknowledge the important contribution the Church makes to national life. In its turn, the Church welcomes the Queen or her representative with due courtesy and signs of civic loyalty. The Lord High Commissioner simply attends the Assembly and listens to the debates. He or she does not take part in these debates or influence decisions.

We nearly added to that sentence 'any more than the man in the public gallery'. It is true, the man in the public gallery can neither vote nor speak in the Assembly but he and his companions throughout Scotland influence the Church more than might be thought. In the last resort the Church of Scotland is answerable to opinion among her members. For example, in recent years there has been a strong current of opinion for reunion within the Christian Church. After long discussion a plan was produced for reunion between the Church of Scotland and the Church of England. This involved the introduction of bishops into the Presbyterian framework of Scottish church government. So far as the man in the street was concerned this meant handing over authority, and the end of the democratic character of the Scottish Church. Nationalist feeling was also involved, for although the majority of Scots do not want separation from England they resent any move to diminish the individuality of Scotland. *The Scottish Daily Express*, which then had the largest circulation of any newspaper in Scotland, led a campaign against the proposal. Those who led the Church were in favour of it, probably the majority of those active in the Church might have accepted it, but the Assembly threw it out. Public opinion was too strong.

Think about . . .

Do Scottish people remember the history of the Church of Scotland? Should they forget it in the modern world?

If you live in Scotland, try to arrange to visit the public gallery when the Assembly is meeting.

6

Beyond the Parish

Till now we have been looking at the Church of Scotland mainly through the parish and congregation. After all, most spectators only see the Christian Church in terms of the congregation nearest to them. But in the modern world the parish is often little more than a place where our home is. Our schooling, our work, and our leisure interests may be in some other part of the town. Also there are people who do not fit into any community but remain strangers. To reach them the Church must step over the parish boundaries.

Often a man's place of work is a world in itself. His wife and children never enter it, and neither does his church. Industry can have its own qualities, some good and some bad, but it cannot be left untouched by the Christian way. So, in addition to the witness and example of members who work in industry, the Church provides industrial chaplains, ministers who are appointed to work in places like the shipyards of Greenock and Port Glasgow on the lower Clyde. The value of the chaplain's work in bringing management and men together and also listening to each other has been acknowledged by employers and shop stewards

A minister at work.

alike. There is a strong group of Christian men in industry who are determined to see that industrial mission continues actively in their midst.

Shipbuilding is an old industry in Scotland, perhaps a dying industry, but oil is a young and rapidly growing one which has suddenly brought thousands of men and their families into quiet places in the far north. In response to an appeal for help from the local churches, the Church of Scotland sent Dr. Robert Peters to Nigg Bay in Ross where about 3300 men were building oil-rigs. Dr. Peters is not a minister but a metallurgist. It is hoped that the Roman Catholic Church and the Scottish Episcopal Church will provide colleagues to work with him.

In Edinburgh the Netherbow was opened, in the High Street, next door to John Knox's House, in time for the Edinburgh Festival of 1974. Among its facilities are a courtyard for open-air performances and a coffee house. Through the winter it is used by groups associated with the churches and the arts and for exhibitions, its purpose being to provide a centre where Christians can express their faith through the arts, and to be a meeting place where the professional arts and the Church may come to a better understanding and appreciation of each other.

Evangelism goes on wherever people go on holiday. There is usually a chaplain at Butlin's Holiday Centre at Heads of Ayr. At Seton Dene camp on the East Lothian shore evangelism is in the hands of young people, for the most part. At Crieff in Perthshire St. Ninian's Training Centre runs a succession of courses for young people learning to share in Christian witness. Activities of this kind are too numerous to list.

For long it was the Scottish Church and not the government that was responsible for education and the care of the poor and disabled. With the coming of the industrial revolution the burden became too heavy for any but the state. Education was largely in the hands of the Church until 1872, but the care of the poor was taken from the Church in 1845. A tradition of Christian compassion survives and is active today. The Church has long worked among the drop-outs of society in the model lodging houses. These grow fewer in number. More recently it has intensified its work among drug addicts and alcoholics. For years the Gorbals Group lived in that depressed and now vanishing Glasgow slum to give a Christian witness. Its leader, the Rev. Geoffrey Shaw, has now become leader of the Strathclyde Regional Council, responsible for the local government of half the population of Scotland. Chaplains serve in the prisons, ministers in the men's prisons and deaconesses in the women's. All this is in one sense thankless work; it brings no visible reward and is undertaken as part of Christian service to the community.

There are other forms of compassion for the very young and the very old. The Church has always been concerned with the plight of children who have no normal home life. It has nine homes in which such boys and girls can grow up in a Christian family setting, cared for by a married couple. The present writer knew a family where a mother died leaving six young children; within a week a home was found for all. There is also a children's holiday home and one which gives holidays to mentally handi-capped children. At the other end of life, the Church has forty-six homes for the elderly who are unable to live by themselves. In between there are many agencies to care for the lonely and those in trouble.

Where specifically religious work is done the Church must depend on its own resources, but much of its work in social welfare is possible nowadays because of the financial support given by government departments and friendly organisations outside the Church.

There was a time when the thoughts of the Scottish Church hardly passed beyond the Scottish border, but in the modern world that is no longer possible. Ever since communications opened with Asia and Africa the Scottish Church has been aware of its share of responsibility for taking the faith to lands that do not know it. When Scottish missionaries are mentioned the name of David Livingstone immediately comes to mind. But Livingstone, though all Scots are proud of him, was not a member of the Church of Scotland but a Congregationalist.

In Victorian times all the Presbyterian Churches now united in the Church of Scotland sent missionaries overseas. Mary Slessor came from the United Presbyterian Church. Once a mill girl in Dundee, this remarkable woman arrived at Calabar in tropical Nigeria in 1876. Her first twelve years were spent with older missionaries at Duke Town, near the coast, and in the Old Town of Calabar. By this time, at home in the language and familiar with the ways of the people, she had decided to move further inland into untouched territory, where life was appallingly primitive and cruel.

At Okoyong, where she settled, a chief had died some months previously, and with him had been buried eight slave men, eight slave women, twenty boys and girls, and four free wives. Twin babies were usually killed at birth. As she set out for this grim field of service by canoe in a tropical downpour an African youth observed that she was courting death.

At first she had to live in one of the women's compounds. Next she built a mud house to her own design, then a church, and a school. Often she was called to help the sick and dying, to save the life of twins, or to still a riot. Her life contradicts the common idea of Victorian women limited to humdrum domestic routine. Like Livingstone she recognised that the development of crafts and commerce was essential for any advance in civilisation. So she persuaded the chiefs to open up relations with the coast and start trading.

Nigeria became a British Protectorate in 1893, not by conquest, but with the consent of the local chiefs. With the coming of British rule cruel customs were suppressed, trade increased, and justice was enforced. Mary Slessor and her companions found themselves accepted and trusted. When she returned from furlough in 1892 she found that she had been appointed a vice-president of the native court at Ikotobong.

West of the Cross River, a tributary of the Niger, was a more primitive countryside where slavery, human sacrifice, and cannibalism were still found. In 1902 a government expedition imposed some order. There was now an opportunity to extend the work, but the mission council considered that its resources were already too stretched. Mary Slessor forced its hand by spending her next furlough, not in Scotland, but in the new territory. She was allowed to remain. In all this she was the pattern of the pioneering missionary in primitive surroundings, supported by the Church at home, but very much an individualist.

Her converts increased, congregations were formed, simple schools and churches were built, and a medical mission was begun at Itu. In 1915, when she died, she left almost fifty churches and schools behind her. Since then, every aspect of the Church has grown in strength in Calabar.

In 1926 a leper arrived at Itu and was received. Others soon followed. From this there grew a great leper colony with four 'towns', farm lands, schools with six hundred children, a babies' home, Scouts and Guides, and its own church, a place where lepers were no longer hopeless and doomed outcasts, but members of a community and with good prospects of cure.

The Church in what once was Calabar, and is now known as Biafra, is passing into a new era where paternalism and depen-

Aspects of the Church's work in Madras:
(above) feeding the children; (below) baptising a family.

dence have ended and partnership has taken their place. The Christian community, which has links with Episcopalians and Methodists as well as with Scottish Presbyterians, is no longer a mission relying on Europeans but a Church of the people, rapidly becoming able to stand on its own feet. Education spreads and standards of living are transformed, and all this despite the ordeal of the Biafran war.

This is characteristic of a widespread change in the overseas missions of the Church. One field after another has become increasingly independent as the local Church grows in strength. Missionaries no longer remain ministers or elders of the Scottish Church but are in the ranks of the local Church and subject to its discipline.

Scottish missions have been established in India, some in cities such as Bombay, Calcutta, and Madras, others in country districts, and in what became Pakistan.

There are others in Jamaica, South Africa, Malawi, Zambia, Kenya, and Ghana. In some of these countries primitive agricultural conditions are being rapidly replaced by industrialism, as in the African copper belt. Almost all are under governments keenly aware of their new independence. In South Arabia, where the Church is tiny, reports from Aden tell of many reforms, but under a Moslem government the Church cannot meet publicly. In South Africa the Scottish mission, which works with the Bantu Presbyterian Church, has troubled relations with a government which is Christian but which dislikes the missions' opposition to apartheid. There is a threat to close the seminary where ministers are trained and Scottish members of staff are liable to be excluded.

So the old image of the missionary as a lone preacher among heathen is outdated. The Scottish Church still has ministers in the overseas missions, but it also has men with the practical skills which are needed as the young Churches pass into the modern world. It provides teachers and professors, nurses, doctors, and pharmacists, accountants, agriculturalists, and technical workers, men and women with skill in literature, publishing, broadcasting, and youth organisation. If the Church of Scotland is a national

Church, its horizons are not narrow; it is part of the world Church in the twentieth century.

Think about . . .

Try to find out more about the various kinds of outreach of the Church of Scotland by contacting the Home Board and the Overseas Mission Department at 121 George Street, Edinburgh.

Important Dates

397	Traditional date for St Ninian, the first recorded Christian in Scotland.
563	Coming of St Columba to Iona.
1067	Coming of St Margaret, whose sons reshaped the Scottish Church.
1560	Scotland becomes Protestant at the Reformation.
1581	The first Presbyteries formed.
1638	The National Covenant.
1688	The Church of Scotland becomes Presbyterian again.
1843	The Disruption: the Free Church leaves the Church of Scotland.
1900	The Free Church and the United Presbyterians unite in the United Free Church.
1929	The Church of Scotland and the United Free Church unite.

Further Reading

You never understand a Church merely by reading about it: contact your local church and find out what it means to its people. However, if you live outside Scotland you will probably have to learn about the Church of Scotland from books. All the statistics of the Church will be found in *The Church of Scotland Yearbook* (Saint Andrew Press), and full accounts of many activities in *Reports to the General Assembly*, popularly known as 'the blue book'. But statistics are the worst possible introduction to any Church. If you cannot attend a service, look at *The Book of Common Order* (Oxford University Press); any volume of *The Daily Study Bible* by William Barclay (Saint Andrew Press) will give you a picture of the faith of the Church of Scotland today.

What Do You Know About the Church? by EDWIN S. TOWILL (Saint Andrew Press).

The Scots Confession of 1560 (Saint Andrew Press).

The Church Hymnary (Oxford University Press, 3rd edition).

The Scottish Parish Kirk by IAN G. LINDSAY (Saint Andrew Press).

The Architecture of Scottish Post-Reformation Churches by GEORGE HAY (Oxford University Press).

The Claims of the Church of Scotland by G. D. HENDERSON (Hodder and Stoughton).

A Church History of Scotland by J. H. S. BURLEIGH (Oxford University Press).

The Scottish Church, 1688–1843 by A. L. DRUMMOND and J. BULLOCH (Saint Andrew Press).

The Church in Victorian Scotland by A. L. DRUMMOND and J. BULLOCH (Saint Andrew Press).

Vision and Achievement, 1796–1956 by ELIZABETH G. K. HEWAT (Thomas Nelson and Sons). A history of the foreign missions of the churches united in the Church of Scotland.

Life and Work is the monthly magazine of the Church of Scotland and *The Bush* is a monthly paper published by GLASGOW PRESBYTERY. Both these may be had from The Church of Scotland Bookshop, 119, George Street, Edinburgh, as may most of the books listed here. The offices of The Church of Scotland are at 121 George Street, Edinburgh. Enquiries should be addressed to the Secretary, The Publicity Committee, at that address.

The Department of Education of the Church of Scotland has recently published a series of handbooks for young people. These include

Exploring in the Church, I and II. (For those aged 12–13.)

Advancing in the Church, I and II. (For those aged 14–15.)

Starting Points. Love. Encountering God. Guide to Resources. (For young adults.)

Commitment in the Church. (For Communicants' Classes.)